The Crown Ain't Worth Much

The Crown Ain't Worth Much

Hanif Abdurraqib

Button Poetry / Exploding Pinecone Press
Minneapolis, Minnesota
2016

Published by Button Poetry / Exploding Pinecone Press
Minneapolis, MN 55403

http://buttonpoetry.com

Manufactured in the United States of America

Cover Art: Max Sansing

Cover Design: Nikki Clark

ISBN 978-1-943735-04-4

23 22 21   6 7 8 9 10

For the mother who raised me. For the city that raised me when she no longer could.

ON HUNGER

And I say now what I have always known:

a king is only named such after the blood of anyone who is not them pools at their feet and grows to be a child's height before running down a hill, flecking the grass of a village crowded with quivering mothers and their boys, huddled underneath a new and undone black sky.

There is not a way to rule without knowing where your family will get its next meal — rather, who it will be taken from, or who will become it. The dead, we know, do not hunger for anything but stillness. Perhaps a memory of them sung around a fire by those still living, their gold worn atop the head of the man who made a widow of their lover.

Consider, though, the wild. The lion that fears nothing and falls into rest with a stomach fat as a second moon. If a lion walks with his head high through the open savanna, the bloody and

detached leg of a hyena swaying from his jaws, he will not be hunted by any animal he cannot render immovable. Will not be attacked by any limbs that he cannot turn into

an undone puzzle, spilled across a playroom floor. When there is no one waiting to dig your chest into a parched well, no army surging over the hills, what is a king but

a heavy name, pulled over a heap of arrogant flesh? The pack of ravenous wolves pray only to the God of survival, its hand as impartial and fleeting as any other

God we build and let carry us to all manner of war. Imagine if there was only one land. If the continents never shook themselves free of each other's touch and still

laid atop each other, the jungle rolling into the desert with no river to divide them. Imagine the pack of wolves running into dusk and setting upon the golden flesh

of a lone lion, roaming the ground he rules. Each wolf climbing atop the other to find their taste. To pierce the neck, stake a set of teeth into a flailing paw until they

have had their jaws lined with nourishment, leaving only a severed head, entrails stretching over the dry land. The wolves would move on, newly throned

and full. Each with a blood prize falling from their mouths, darkness running over the new Earth. Every animal that watched, cheering a vicious king's corpse in the high grass. The clouds may weep for this, wash away another dead thing.

But I imagine all of this in a world where the wolves do not have to lose any of their own to be fed. Where the food they desire comes, trembling, to even their smallest

children. Where they have a homeland.

Don't have to run into every untethered

night howling into the emptiness.

The old man rocks / on the porch and tells us / boys that the way to power is / displaying what you kill / letting a body rot in the stink / of summer's blaze / meat cooked dark on / the steaming pavement / so that no one will dare hunt / you while you sleep / or / so a mother knows where / to collect whatever / is left of / her lineage and / push it under her tongue / until it swells / fat with grief / in the hood / everyone is driven to kill / by some kind of distinct / famine / a family pressed up / against each other's exposed ribs / what a luxury it must be / to hand over death / for the sake of watching someone die / to not have to answer for the blood / you have spilled / until the gates of heaven ask / about the history of your palms / I don't know how my people / navigated their land before / they were shook free from its touch / and thrown down in / a hot field with new / names and / new songs of survival to / fit into their bulging mouths / but I think of the nights / thick with the pounding of black / footsteps and the distant / howling of flames as / I watch the burning of another building / in a city soaked by / a death which fed / no one's hunger / the fire rising to kiss the / black belly of a night sky / each star a set of / gleaming and eager / teeth

TABLE OF CONTENTS

On Hunger

I

II

III

I was learning the importance of names — having them, making them — but at the same time I sensed the dangers. Recognition was followed by oblivion, a yawning maw whose victims disappeared without a trace.

Josephine Baker

The crown ain't worth much if the nigga wearin' it always gettin' his shit took.

Marlo Stanfield

†.

I'm from a place where the church is the flakiest /
niggas is praying to god so long that they Atheist

Jay-Z

AT MY FIRST PUNK SHOW EVER, 1998

me & tyler jump into the pit head first even though four older boys
got patches that say *NO BLACKS* & *NO QUEERS* & I flinch &
cover my head when the drum kicks too sharp & I don't know
what could be more black than that & tyler don't know it but in an
alley last month I saw him build a church in the mouth of a boy
from 'cross town who don't talk to nobody & don't come 'round
the hood unless he thirsty for a tithe but we up in the pit anyway
'cuz it ain't the 70s anymore what I mean is there ain't a war always
on television what I mean is we came here to see blood like all boys
who sneak past their sleeping fathers & crawl out of windows
before running into the night with ripped jeans & ain't all blood the
same when bodies get hurled like they in a cheap amusement park
ride & some blond girl from bexley gets slick & tries to sneak into
the rampage but not before tyler & some other boy grab her by the
collar & toss her smooth out & then they high five & through the
guitar bending over our heads like an umbrella I hear tyler whisper
some things are just unacceptable & then he puts his head in his hands &
his whole body begins to shake & I tell myself it can only be
laughter

IN DEFENSE OF "MOIST"

Sprawling river / peeling off the chest / a wet slap / endless summer / not quite drenched to the bone / yet still a burden / how it sits heavy on the tongue / after being spoken / leaving the mouth / a humid storm / becoming the definition of itself / inside you / heaviness in the prison of your chest / I am trying to pull my shirt over my head / after a full court game / in June / and I am thinking of how everyone I love / was once taken from the inside of another person / *moist* with what carried them / into the world / isn't that worth the smallest praise / I am closing my eyes / as the shirt's cotton clings to my back / and I am thinking that all wetness must have teeth / especially the wetness that grows from within / and spills out / or / chews its way through the skin / and falls onto another's skin / the night Michael Jackson died / everyone black / in Ohio / danced in a basement / until the walls were *moist* / until it rained indoors / and we saw our heroes / resurrected in the reflection / of our own drowning / I say *moist* / and do not first think about two naked bodies / the sound their skin might make / when they awkwardly press into each other / underneath a hungry sun / in an apartment with a broken air conditioner / I say *moist* / and first think of / the eager and swallowing mud / the bullet that burrowed into Sean's chest / on Livingston Ave / the country of dark red / that grew across his white tee / while his mother held / his paling face / I say *moist* / as in / *my homie's blood left the corner of my block moist* / or / *his mama had her hands moist with what once kept her baby alive* / or / *my eyes were moist when I heard the o.g. say* / *"niggas gonna die every day"* / and then he wiped blood off of his shoe / and it felt like summer for ten years

4

WHEN WE WERE 13, JEFF'S FATHER LEFT THE NEEDLE DOWN ON A JOURNEY RECORD BEFORE LEAVING THE HOUSE ONE MORNING AND NEVER COMING BACK

and this is why none of us sing along to "Don't Stop Believin'" when we are being driven by Jeff's mom, four boys packed in the backseat tight like the tobacco in them cigarettes Jeff's mom got riding

shotgun with us around I-270 in a powder blue Ford Taurus where four years later Jeff will lose his virginity to a girl behind the East High School football field then later that night his keys and pants in the school pool so that he has to run

home crying to his mother with an oversized shirt and no pants, like a cartoon bear, and the next day when I hear this story, I will think about what it means for someone to become naked two times in one night to rush into the warmth of two

women, once becoming a man and once becoming a boy all over again but right now it is just us in this car with Jeff's mother, that cigarette smoke dancing from her lips until it catches the breeze

from the cracked front window and glides back towards us a vagabond, searching for a throat to move into and cripple while Neal Schon's guitar rides out the speakers and I don't know how many open windows a man has to climb out of in the middle of the night in order to have hands that can make anything scream like that.

nothing knows the sound of abandonment like a highway does, not even God.

in the 1980s, everyone wrote songs about someone leaving except for this one cuz it's about how the morning explodes over two people in one bed who didn't know each other the night before when alone

was the only other option and their homes had too many mirrors for all that shit and so it is possible that this is the only song written in the 1980s about how fear turns into promise
I think I know this because there is so much piano spilling

all over our laps that we can't help but to smile since we still black and know nothing can ransack sorrow like a piano.

Jeff's mother's hand trembles and still wears a wedding ring so she pulls over to the side of the highway and turns the volume up so loud after the second guitar solo when the keys kick in again that we can barely hear the cocktail

of laughter and crying consuming the front seat until the song fades away and the radio is low again and the ring once on Jeff's mother's hand is on the side of the highway beneath us, a sacrifice

and so maybe this is why grandma said a piano can coax even the most vicious of ghosts out of a body.

and so maybe this is why my father would stare at the empty spaces my mother once occupied, sit me down at a baby grand and whisper *play me something, child.*

SEPTEMBER, JUST EAST OF THE JOHNSON PARK COURTS

if the kicks on your feet are clean and sharp
as the carved moon when a tall boy asks
what size you wear, cuz? and bends
to meet your face until the hunger in his eyes
renders you a lighter shade of black
stirs the sleeping crows from your skin
and sends them howling
into another brave and unshaken body
you will walk home dragging your bare feet
through a terrace of bottles that were full
and unbroken when the men nodding off
in their beach chairs and stained with the stink
of desolation needed something to help them
forget their waking hours as the sun heaved itself free this morning
what was left of late summer's
stolen warmth spilling from its arms
and you take the long way and walk slow
because your father is waiting
and knows what it is to grow up poor
what it is to take something another man has earned
he will carry you by your sweaty collar to the tall boy's front yard
and you will not leave with your shoes
but you will leave a man
the husk of your boyhood snapped under the weight
of another's fists beating the cries for a buried decaying
mother from your tongue
the heel of shoes that you claimed
just an hour ago pressing into your neck
while every father on the block gathers to watch
another bloody bar mitzvah another destitute boy
learning what it is to suffocate
someone with their own gold

ALL THE GANG BANGERS FORGOT ABOUT THE DRIVE-BY

no one wants to see the block party broken up
right when their jam cracks open and drips from the speakers
but no one wants to bleed out during a hot and unforgiving
    summer either
we all have to make sacrifices
we all have to keep the dirt from underneath the fingernails of our
    mothers
even if it means not getting to wrap our hands around the swaying
    waist
of Britney from algebra class
who has a forest of thick braids that stretch almost to her running
    legs
nothing produces movement like the gun
how two shots kissing the feet of an undressing sky
can turn the dance floor   into a thirsty mouth
faster than the streetlights and the calls rising from the project
    windows
It is what I know will always come once the heat moves in
and ransacks the calm body of spring
there is no song   that can press its shoulder against this door
there is only the dark alley shepherding you home
there is only the boombox that has lived longer than your
    neighbor's child
there is only the cd inside its back red and scratched
like it was tied to the whipping post
and forced to skip in the same spot every night
it plays:

you see the hood's been good to me
you see the hood's been good
you see the hood
you see the hood

     you see

ODE TO DRAKE, ENDING WITH BLOOD IN A FIELD

yeah we finally learned how / to undress a whole season / with just our tongues / & pull back the sheets / with its taste / still in our mouths / & that'll do 'til / our lovers come back / or 'til we find one / who will take us / despite our flaws & / how we can't stop building monuments / to all of them / so that we never have / to apologize to anyone / not for all of / the gold / or the backwards / hats & new walk / in every city like / we run shit / but mufuckas never / loved us / they'll never forget / about the teen dramas / mine weren't on tv / so I don't need tattoos / but I also curse / more on the eastside these days / I don't want to be threatening / just feared / enough to never have to / make a fist / I learned this when / the dj got dragged / out his whip after / the block party for / playing too much marvin gaye / & not enough mobb deep / 'cuz make love / when the time is right / but we still hood / don't you ever / get it fucked up / & have you heard / what they say about men / who have swallowed / decades of summer? / & how they will come / for us with broken glass / in their teeth / & carry us on / their backs / to where the grass be / taller than them project buildings / once was / & they will cut open / our stomachs & / wear our sunlight / around their shoulders / like a mother's arms / & summer won't end / until after they have / forgotten the flags we planted.

THE SUMMER A TRIBE CALLED
QUEST BROKE UP

all them black
    boys in the 'hood
        had they wallets
           unearthed in cities
              they ain't never
         seen before & they
           was all empty
        'cept for maybe the bones
     of the last woman
   to hold them in her arms &
call them by the
name they blessed the
earth with & all of the horns
    on my block crawled back
       into they cases & marched to
         new mouths & fathers
         had nothing to press
         their lips to & make sing &
      i think this why brandon's mother
    left & what difference is there
in those things which we lose
& those things which decide
to gift us with a kind
   of feral silence?
     the change that leapt
      from our pockets into the cracked
       basketball courts & the older brothers

      who never found their way back home

1995. AFTER THE STREETLIGHTS DRINK WHATEVER DARKNESS IS LEFT

we stop throwin up jump shots cuz the rim seen better days
  whole hood seen better days
    whole hood bent & cracked & been
      held together on a prayer despite the shallow bricks &
      the homie says *these the hours where black boys vanish*
      says *we gotta find shelter before teeth grow through all this twilight*
      says *one time I looked up at the moon and I haven't seen my big brother*
      since
      says *I guess this skin we wear expires with the sun*
      says *we were born into curfew* & I think
        what a way to be young & alive
          but then we hear the vibrant song of sirens cutting through
          the night
            & even as boys our legs know to carry us to someone's
            grandma's crib
          & we don't yet know why & we don't yet understand
          the way
            a grandmother's arms linger around our fragile limbs
            for a few seconds
              longer when we finally make it home breathing & in
              the winter
            danny lost track of time shooting free throws
              & we had to bury all of the parts of him that the
              night left,
                still brimming with bullets & then
                none of the black boys
                  got new basketballs for
                                    christmas.

11

XVI

didn't nobody's mama's / mama / bite clean through the meat /
of their bottom lip / while on they knees / in the corner of some
white man's kitchen / so their grandbaby could mow lawns / for
four dollars an hour / during a hot and infinite summer / 'til they
hands became a poppy field / of blisters /

but oh well / god knows / we work 'til we fly / god knows
grandma worked / 'til sudden wings grew out her back / and now
sunday dinners ain't the same / pops ain't left the bedroom since
july / when I got enough money for those new jordans / and it
rained for two weeks / straight / we so Midwest / we so pretty
sunrise / but bet there be a storm later / bet some thunder rattles
the walls /

so I walk past them white air force ones / I'm on that all black shit
again / I'm on that all my flaws be glowing when I'm held to the
light shit again / but at least I clean up easy / at least I can run
into a storm / and cover all manner of sins / at least I can wear
these 'til winter rides over the hills / and settles on the front porch
/ or 'til all that snow melt / and I gotta walk through franklin park
to get to jasmine house / cuz she love how fresh I got since last
school year / now I got the whole hood grasping for this fly / got
my kicks sinking / into the wet mud / got ancestors grabbing at
my feet from their graves

DISPATCHES FROM THE BLACK BARBERSHOP, TONY'S CHAIR, 1996.

*we all know a couple niggas doin a bid derrick ain't comin home for another
20 cuz he shot up westside trevor's whip after trevor slapped his baby's mom yo
tuck your lip so I can get this beard anyway trevor ain't die at least not that
night but someone gonna have to catch his ass slippin we from the streets we
ain't just gonna let niggas put hands on women we ain't just gonna let niggas
keep their hands we all got mamas you know but I don't fuck with guns no
more I got babies now you dig tilt your head into the light for me anyway yeah I
got babies my nigga derrick ain't gonna see his babies til they too heavy to lift
til they forget that he got a body that don't live in front of glass goddamn bruh
I can't be out here like that I got to eat I got to make this money I can't give
nobody a reason to wear my face on a tshirt you feel me police already want a
nigga in a metal box or or a wooden box I ain't gonna let myself get buried I
saw derrick's baby's mom on east courtright digging a hole in the mud with her
bare hands till they cracked wide open hold still I accidentally cut a nigga
yesterday cuz he wouldn't stop moving the blood ain't stop for like four hours
the blood was everywhere the blood was a river the blood ran on to the street
was like that shit had legs I ain't seen that much blood since I last fell asleep in
my girl's arms I ain't seen that much blood since my first son was born and all
the dreams I been havin since*

I DON'T REMEMBER THE WHOLE SUMMER WHEN "DO THE RIGHT THING" DROPPED

but I do remember the night that police got a hold of Big Mike from North Linden & beat his face into the sweltering brick outside what used to be a Pizza Hut until it got robbed by some southside stickup kids two summers earlier & then my big brother said it had to shut down cuz niggas ain't gonna get a gun held to they head for minimum wage & Mike used to deliver pizzas to the hood before the hood woke up in winter with new hungers & come spring, Mike was rockin' a gold rope 'round his neck thicker than the coils in a hangman's knot & that's when the cops on the eastside began to lick their lips & when their hands started to tremble while whispering 'bout what they would do to him if they ever caught his ass, which maybe explains the way his bright blood painted the abandoned brick & the five police still pressing their heels into his face even after his right eye swung free from its socket, a grisly pendulum & my big brother left me home alone & hungry that night when the whole hood ran from their homes and set upon the police with any weapon they could find & they say that Mike's face was a bloody & wet mess & they say he wasn't breathing or they say he ain't have a mouth anymore or they say all of him was a dark & gaping hole & they say the police grew fangs & they say the thick fur pushed through their shirts while Mike bled & earlier that day, my big brother hid his white jordans in his bookbag when he came back to the hood from his suburban job & he walked in the door & said we all one handful of gold away from a closed casket funeral & I don't know how many mothers walked from the mouth of that summer childless but I could see the old Pizza Hut burning from my window & I could see a cop being dragged into the bushes by the stickup kids & isn't it funny how art most imitates life when a black body is being drained of it? how easily we can imitate that which is never coming back again to claim its space? & when my big brother came home that night, he carried me to bed with a glass of warm milk & when a drop of

blood fell from his knuckles & blended into the white of the glass,
I did not ask who it belonged to.

WINDSOR TERRACE, 1990

Around the flickering old box that Jason's granddad lifted from the corner of Aven and Barnett, we huddle our limbs to watch Mike Tyson's legs become stiff oak

before he falls at the feet of Buster Douglas, who used to live right over there on Linden. Where, legend has it, he dunked so hard in a high school game that the air felt like a spaceship

took off right here in the streets and the ground ain't stopped vibrating since. Some nights, we press our bodies to it and feel the hum run through the dark fat of our small legs,

rise and tell our mothers we can fill their fists with gold one day, buy our way out of this persistent stew of cold and sleeplessness.

On the television, Tyson is crawling around on the canvas like I've seen a man crawl on the living room floor, praying for enough change to keep a baby's modest stomach

full for another night and maybe these two things are both a survival of violence. A man is shown his own blood and plummets to the earth

before trying to force himself to rise once more. When people pay money to watch, we call this sport. When people spill from their apartments

into a dim alley or a decaying school yard to watch, we call this the ghetto. But the cheering is the same. The excitement one gets in watching legs

that are not their own twitching in the dirt has never left us, ever since we watched the first funeral roll slow down the block.

And now Tyson is trying to force his mouthpiece between his unhinged and begging mouth while reaching for the ropes and

16

Jason's grandfather's trembling voice is whispering

get up boy, goddamn.
get up just one more time.

and he is almost looking past the television, into the night.

AIN'T NONE OF THE KIDS ON MY BLOCK GONNA DEBATE ABOUT THE EXISTENCE OF GOD

cuz
this 1 time
summer '91 MJ jumped
From   way out
n stayed

                                     up there

so long swear we
thought grandpa
finally got sober
but he still smellin
like the sweat you
get from trynna
outrun some real heavy
shit that done finally caught
yo ass n MJ showin
James Worthy the rock in
one hand but then he
take it away n James lookin
like he just lost his mama in
the grocery store or
some shit but MJ still   up there

                                  n ain't nobody else
                                  wit 'em so we all packed close to
                                  the TV n when he finally

                                  come down

                                  Brandon big cousin
                                  (who used to be showing
                                  the whole hood
                                  the rock

n how to get high
n never come down)
flushed his stash
down the toilet
n grabbed a ball
said "you lil niggas the Lakers"
n swear to god he flew
til the sun came up

ODE TO KANYE WEST IN TWO PARTS, ENDING IN A CHAIN OF MOTHERS RISING FROM THE RIVER

I wake up the morning after another award show and I hear
the calls surging over the mountains again
I hear 'em
saying

hey
boy
you know we ain't
rupture this country's spine and unearth all its gold for you people to cocoon
your teeth in it
let your mouths spill all over our sacred trophies get fingerprints on the gilded
bark
of crowns
our men earn and set in the fire until they melt down into the bright and flesh of
another woman who will never cup your face
in her hands
and sing into your ear while the certain darkness of night turns chicago to a
muted child
you ain't getting that again 'til heaven calls for your body
after it been tied to a truck in east texas
by another diamond drowned jesus chain
and dragged through that jagged metal holy land so you can meet god clean

open and split
just give us your neck and we will carry you back to the sound
of your
mama's voice

•

when I say I wanted the boy who cursed my dead mother's name to become a ghost, I mean I wanted the bones of him to rattle on his father's nightstand. I wanted another man to wake up haunted as the men who christened every morning screaming into the shell of whatever buried love still lived in the wood of the only home they could afford and isn't that also another language for grief? there are only so many ways to dream about a corpse before you find new things to call *sleep*, or a new thing worth closing   your eyes for the woman pulling you to the warmth of her living mouth or Nina Simone's voice laid tight and naked over something your boys can rap to until there is enough money to move out the hood and into somewhere not creased with songs of the lifeless. Somewhere with food for everyone, even if it ain't the fish our mothers cooked on Sundays, the smell of it crawling in under our bedroom doors and folding us in its arms. When I say I wanted the boy who cursed my dead mother's name to become a ghost I mean I wanted the bones of uncooked fish to rattle in his throat while everyone he loved watched with their hands pressed underneath their chairs. I think I'm better now. I still watch a couple dance with their smiling children in a park and I want to tell them how easy it is for all of us to wake up next to someone who never will again. I am like you. I still want to feast on the happiest moments of strangers. I don't know what this makes men like us except bound to our loneliness, crawling on our hands and knees again through the southern mud that women we loved once pushed between their black toes, until we reach the river. press our lips to the bank. whisper their names into the delicate brown earth and pray the water parts this time. Every mother we gave over to death, walking from its cool mouth. A wet and thrashing catfish in their arms. They will ask

have you eaten, child?
you closed your eyes
during another one of my sweet songs
and I thought you would
never   wake

ALL OF THE BLACK BOYS
FINALLY STOPPED PACKING
SWITCHBLADES

since the summer of '98 when
danny went into the pit and got his front teeth
divorced from the rest of his mouth by the fist
of some white boy from the side of town
where no one buries a boy that came into the world
after they did and no one ever has to swallow
their own blood and pray that it will keep them
fed until morning
so danny told us that he was going to
go home with someone's teeth even if they weren't
the ones that he came here with
because how many things have we boys had ripped
from our mouths and never replaced by anyone?
how much of our language has been pulled over the tongues
of everyone but us?
reparations were sought in dark alleys with a blade sharp
enough to scare a jaw open and a prayer out of a sinner's
mouth which explains how the white boy wept
and called for his father when being pressed
into the brick with danny's foot against his neck while
we watched until danny finally let the boy
go and we ran back out east towards our homes and maybe
it was the way the rain howled or maybe where
we come from we see everything drowning in red anyway
or maybe there is no other way to explain the haste with which I
make my pockets barren before leaving the house
even today
or why my wife needs a bigger purse to carry such weight
for the both of us
but when the police came for us that night
we did not hear a sound until danny's blade fell out his pocket
and the bullets that followed
because I guess anything can be a gun if the darkness

surrounding it is hungry enough
or at least that's what I've been told when
the bodies of black boys thrash against what
little life they have left tethering them to the earth
and isn't that what we've always been fed? that it is
just like the nighttime
to rename everything that moves
into a monster?

ON JUKEBOXES

the ones on sheridan ave stopped playing motown in the fall once
the frat boys found out they could drink for cheap & stumble
down the block loud & pulsating with the night the way our fathers
used to when this side of town was still thick with their fingerprints
& so we take the cash we won over on the north courts, where
jason ain't missed a jump shot since his big brother got outta
prison & started to slow dance with them corners again, & we go
to the quik mart to buy some quarter water that don't quench
anything except our desire to be black & young & spend the money
we earned with our own sweat & I think something about that is
also black & our parents ain't seen us since morning stretched over
the hood & all these decaying rooftops but we still hop in tyler's
mama's ford & go down to sheridan ave to see the old head who
sits outside monk's bar with a newport forever swinging from his
bottom lip so low it defy gravity & for the right price, he been
known to sing whatever marvin gaye song he's sober enough to
remember & so we take what change we got left & put it in his cup
& he starts in on some marvin & the words *"brother, brother, brother /
there's far too many of you dying"* crawl out from his lips & grow legs &
a whole body right there on the sidewalk & it wraps itself around
us & jason is bent over & heaving & I try not to look & tell myself
that it's because we played eight games straight earlier & summer
came through the hood this year & decided to stay too long & wear
out its welcome like tyler's grandma in his family's 2-bedroom
apartment but that's why he been staying at my crib lately & I think
to tell my boys we should go back there before we run into
midnight & the questions that come with it & before I can say
anything some capital university kids run up & take the old head's
change cup & run away yelling *this ain't the side of town for y'all anymore*
& when I get accepted there in the winter, me & jason stop talking.

†† .

I've read about the afterlife, but I've never really lived.

Pete Wentz

THE YEAR MY BROTHER STOPPED LISTENING TO HIP-HOP

I was 19
& four girls went missing
from the rusted swing set beside scottwood elementary
where we used to throw basketballs at the bent
rim with no net after dark
& Trenton
who was once young & stole
kisses from high school girls
underneath the Bishop Hartley bleachers
got arrested for pulling
a .45 in the club because it was Saturday night &
the *N* word crawled out
from behind the wrong tongue &
swam through the bass right before the beat
dropped & someone always gotta throw fists
into something sacred after last call
& it was still eastside
& *we still so hood*
& Jay-Z called himself *Hova*
twelve times in one song
which blared from the speakers in my first apartment
so loudly I couldn't hear my father when he asked why
I didn't come to the mosque anymore
& I got a ticket for my window tint being too dark
& maybe my skin bearing too much of a resemblance on
a backstreet in Bexley but I lied & told my grandmother
it was for speeding so that I could stay fly
& my new nephew howled into the world on the same day
Biggie would have turned 30 so I was late
to the hospital because it was almost summer in the Midwest
& *mo' money mo' problems* was on the radio at sunset &
I was cruising down Livingston
with a girl riding shotgun who woke up
that morning in my Tribe Called Quest t-shirt hoping
I would finally tell her I loved her back

29

& two months later she fell in love with a coast
where my phone calls were no longer currency
& I didn't know how to define *that kind of* alone
so that year I spent my tuition refund check on new headphones
& turned the volume up on everything & slowly
walked into the water

DUDES, WE DID NOT GO THROUGH THE HASSLE OF GETTING THESE FAKE IDS FOR THIS JUKEBOX TO NOT HAVE ANY SPRINGSTEEN

& it is the end of another summer where I have slept on my couch for days only allowing another body to interrupt long enough for our limbs to tangle like weeds up the side of a brick house, reaching for something impossible. I promise there have always been dishes spilling out of the sink, love. It's how I discovered this kind of hunger. Last week, Rick lit a cigarette & yelled across the bar that the only difference between smoking & kissing someone who smokes is the way mouths collide before death sits in your lungs like an abandoned city & everyone laughed while I tried to wipe another's lip gloss from my cheek. Most people I know cannot sleep until they crawl through someone else's hollow. There are nights when I wish we were all still children, but then again, I suppose we may be or at least there is no other way to explain how we make every doorway our own. The way we stain ourselves & anything else that moves. The way we scream into the dark like a siren & the weeping, yet another thing we never mention in the morning. I think I am starting to vanish slowly from head to toe. There are ten different ways to say *sunset*. The bartender says my face is wearing all of them.

COLLEGE AVENUE, HALLOWEEN, 2002

Earlier, on the floor of my dorm room, Brittany told me

I mean, dude, I know you're Buddy Holly but only because YOU'RE telling me you're Buddy Holly. Everyone at the party may just think you're a black guy in an old suit.

And I told her that she had no idea what she was talking about because this was the 2000s, and we are only 19 and not yet saddled with the burdens of our parents except for in the middle of some nights, when the loneliness slides itself along our necks like a crucifix and we gasp for anything familiar,
but I told her that time is not now, not when this tweed striped jacket was 49.99, and I spent all morning shining these shoes, so clean I could see my face in them, if that face were white which it kind of will be in a way later, I told her, if only in the confidence it will have in itself.

But, right now tonight, everyone at this party thinks I am dressed as Sammy Davis Jr., and the decades old couch I am pushing my fingers in between is wrapped in torn cloth covered like a grandmother's bible the girl next to me curves her spine around the 90s pop song swinging its legs over the air and asks me *where Frank Sinatra is* and I want to ask her what she knows of the Apollo, the Mecca, bowing to four white kids from Lubbock Texas in 1957 if she knows how hard it might be for her to squeeze a standing ovation outta all of those black hands but I smile instead and just say *Frank's buried in California* so she will give me her phone number and I can pretend to have lost it on the hardwood floor of this house which has the consistency and activity of a beehive, all at once sticky and buzzing

so I go outside to escape the coat of dried beer throwing itself over the bare and cracking walls. Outside, my white friend Andy, who sits in the back during documentary film class and wears his pants and fitted cap so low we think he's sleeping, tells me I make a good

Sammy Davis Jr. and I tell him I am supposed to be Buddy Holly,
so he laughs and says *what's the difference*, and I say
a burning plane in an empty field, and a burning cross in front of a house
and then he stops laughing and asks if I saw the girl
dressed as Pocahontas
and I said no at the time but then she was stumbling out of the
previously locked bathroom when I went back inside and she was
followed by Tupac, or at least someone who was once close to
resembling Tupac before this moment when the brown and black
makeup sweats from his previously white skin and he pulls a
feather once belonging to a headdress from his tongue, and stares
at the girl whose taste was still splitting his throat wide open,
and without looking at me he says *Man. there are some things that stay
with you your whole life. there are some things it is impossible to sleep off.*

I promise the girl on the couch I will call her and maybe I will after
all because I am becoming more and more like my father every day,
the way we both swing into the darkness like it is our
birthright, the way we both crave the moon and the breeze dancing
in for the gossip after we walk out of the party, which I do to get
back to the dorm, so I can tell Brittany she was right

up until the corner of College and Ruhl, where back in '75, before
the houses were worth millions, I hear the dealers would kill you
right where you stood for fuckin' with their corner and the police
sirens knew these streets like a second language and still do though
for different reasons, or so they say
as the red and blue glow devours the blackest parts of the night,
and the officers press arms into my back and yell questions which
don't desire answers, the kind of questions that have *nothing to do*
with what I'm doing out at this hour.

On the other end of the sidewalk Andy from documentary film
class and his friends finish their cans of beer and throw them on
someone's lawn before running into the alley, but none of the
officers move, except for when my student ID falls out of my
pocket, and only then, when a flashlight shines on it just long
enough for one of them to get a glimpse,

and when our legs are all once again planted to the pavement, though only mine trembling, and when my jacket is wearing a fresh tear, one officer looks me up and down.

Says,

Sorry. We thought you were someone else.

ALL THE WHITE BOYS ON THE EASTSIDE LOVED LARRY BIRD

cuz he put up his finger to celebrate before the 3 even went in back in '86 / during the 3-point contest / i guess he knew it was good / or i guess he knew he already won / like the white boys in bexley who we would find when there was no food in our kitchens / and play them for whatever money their parents could spare / knowing they couldn't hang / cuz tony and mario just made varsity and we could take their money easy / and they would always get more / their 3-pointers would smack the backboard / the rim a trembling halo / and still their hands raised letting the late summer drink from an underserving fingertip / before they walked home on a street where no one had died / while we took twenty dollars to mcdonalds and got enough food to last the weekend / i know that if i sweat enough i will be fed / or something will be built / but not bear my name when it is finished / i tear open a hamburger and my fingertips are slick with grease / i hold them to the sky but no breeze comes / always the eager mouth / never the hand that feeds / when i scored 20 against watterson / their student section called me a *nigger* / a small price to pay / for my name in the newspaper / a picture of my face / 3 pages past the section where my grandmother checks for funerals / they say to have your name stripped and sewed back together by the same hands / is a kind of victory / where i'm from / none of the black boys celebrate / until the ball slides through the net / falling satisfied from its mouth / this is what waking up without a mother will do / the story about larry bird goes / he walked into a locker room that night and asked / *which one of you is playing for second place?* to a room full of black players / and no one made a sound

THE SCOUTING REPORT FOR THE ONLY BLACK BOY ON THE SOCCER TEAM

says:
he real
fast but he prone to gamble
like his daddy was when
harlem was still loud and
tall and swaying
and they both make the kinda
mistakes that leave whole families
on their backs
in the grass mourning and
hungry
he real fast though and
short but he jump real
real high like there
might be somethin' in
the sky he trying to reach
he jump way higher this season
heard the sky opened up and
got his grandma last winter but
he take plays off
like he out here sleeping
he be sleep through 6am practice
sleep through women's studies class
sleep through his mom's throat
closing shut like an old wound
sleep through the sirens and gasping outside
his bedroom door and barely even
move 'til she a ghost
but he real fast
and see the whole field
sometimes think he
may never stop watching
just waiting for someone
to come home.

ODE TO ELLIOTT SMITH, ENDING IN THE FIRST SNOWFALL OF 2003

& when they come for us & whatever is left of our spectral bodies
tells them that we were always as lonely as we were the day we were
pulled from our mothers, thrashing & cold
when screaming was the only language & therefore it was a gift &
not the burden it is when trying to call out to a lover quickly
evaporating into shadows
as your own blood congregates in your lungs
on the day when the knife grew impatient in its demanding of flesh,
six of us piled into the corner booth at twin palace
& emptied our nearly barren pockets so that we could order two
plates of beef fried rice because
if you pretend to love enough
people

you will never go to bed hungry &
we don't have any money to tip but we leave anyway because other
people's hunger is not our problem once we are fed & we took
extra fortune cookies &
Kristen's said *Drink up, baby. Look at the stars* &
Rick's said *everything you were born with will provide you with infinite*
warmth & we laugh at the starless night sky dressed in thick clouds
& how Rick shivers even though it is only October & the air
is not supposed to settle into our bones with knives
until months from now when we
lie to our families about why we won't
be coming home for Christmas break & Kristen yells
all fortunes are liars at the sky & it answers back
with heavy white powder that licks
at the sidewalks & rests in our hair until we
are covered in this broken promise of stars & warmth
& I look at the discarded fortunes & the broken cookies that
once held them & I wonder if this
is how our parents see us now promising gifts

birthed & pulled from
a loving shell only to grow into another disaster
uninvited & spreading itself along the streets with a
slow crawl & the wind blows one last tiny strip
& it lands on my shoe & says *WE ARE ALL GOING
TO DIE ALONE* & I don't tell anyone the truth
for a whole year

IN DEFENSE OF THAT WINTER WHERE I LISTENED TO THE FIRST TAKING BACK SUNDAY ALBUM EVERY DAY UNTIL THE SNOW PEELED ITSELF BACK FROM THE GRASS AND I FOUND MY COLLEGE SWEATSHIRT AGAIN

We got kicked out of the only bar that could fit us
& all of the sadness we latched to our backs when

Jared swallowed too much of something dark & burning
right before

he took the microphone from someone singing *Beat It* during
karaoke night & started to read a poem he

found in the ice outside our apartment the morning after the
cancer came back & stretched itself wide

in his mother's lungs & all I heard before he got pulled
by the collar was something about *the slow dying of a town*

drowning in its own oil & now we have nowhere to drink
ourselves into whatever silence will make the night into

a time machine. Instead, I give another new girl my warmest
clothes while we stare up at the moon and clutch each other out

of the necessity for warmth & never the hunger for romance.
She asks if I have ever watched a singer throw

his grief over an audience like a blanket, a mass of boys
weeping in the front

row & I tell her yes because I have seen a father singing
a prayer into his palms while a woman he loves

39

fades away forever & I think
this may be the same thing

I think I have been among the mass of boys
crying in the ruins of a city painted in

the cool grey of heartache. Ice is starting
to fall from the sky again.

It falls into the hair of the girl I am holding
& I run my fingers through it,

looking for the end of a poem. She asks
if I have ever watched someone

take a shovel & chisel the ground until it fits only them & what
they can carry in their arms to heaven &

I tell her no even though I can see Jared sitting in the light
from the upstairs window, holding the picture of his mother

where he is small & holding her hands & crying next to a wooden
roller coaster that once stretched high into the Cincinnati

sky but was just torn to dust & replaced
with something metal & fast & howling

because the boys stopped being afraid
& told themselves that they could never die

from anything & I think of this watching Jared in the glow
of his younger self & his living mother & the two cigarettes

he is holding in each hand, drinking the thick
black smoke into his lungs &

closing his eyes in prayer & I don't know if it is love that carries us
to that kind of drowning so I ask the girl I am holding

if she has ever seen a boy so in love with another person
that the boy sews his own burial suit with his bare hands

WHEN I SAY THAT LOVING ME IS KIND OF LIKE BEING A CHICAGO BULLS FAN

what I mean is that my father can tell a bunch of cool stories about back in the day when I was truly great. there is a mountain of gold that has gathered dust in the corner where I used to sleep, and look at all of these pictures. in this one, I am wearing rainbow shorts and hurling rocks at a shoreline. in this one, I am smiling in the glow of 13 lit candles pushed into a sheet of dark sugar. you may ask why I allow my face to drown in less and less joy with each passing year and I will say *I just woke up one day and I was a still photo in everyone else's home but my own.* or I will say *I promise that my legs just need another season, and then I will be who you fell in love with again.* and then probably just *I'm sorry that there was once a tremendous blue sky and then a decade of hard, incessant rain.*

CLUB 185, BEXLEY, 2003

Nick Drake killed himself by overdosing on anti-depressants

29 years ago tonight which no

other soul cares about in this bar

but I have just enough money to search out Pink Moon on the juke

so I do and go to press

play but my roommate Rick who is drunk, and laughing,

and already casting

his heartbreak over every girl in this bar like a dark cloud

says *c'mon man. no one here wants to hear that shit*

so he presses play on "Don't Stop Believin'"

instead and the whole bar locks arms and sings along while I

go outside and lean into the city's first snowfall that year

I watch the skyline huddle and shiver

like I was seeing it from my mother's backseat for

the first time

DISPATCHES FROM THE BLACK BARBERSHOP, TONY'S CHAIR. 2003.

I guess they ain't cuttin' hair in them college towns you lil niggas live in these days damn nigga you got naps reachin for the whole sky bet your mama up there with that black pick she used to chase you down the block with I ain't make the funeral cuz big mike got buried that same day I see you got a little beard now nigga what you think you grown anyway you know niggas gotta choose what funerals we go to these days shit feel like we just moving dirt from on top of one dead body to another feel like heaven just got all our mamas and brothers and them niggas from the corner up there round one big table talkin bout how much they miss the hood you seen that coffee shop they put where ms tammi's soul food spot used to be right down the block ms tammi ain't been the same since her man stopped comin' home last winter you know when all that snow come through some niggas just chase after the sun and don't never come back when they find it but now that coffee shop got all them white folk comin round lift up your chin bro yeah my girl said the hood gonna be alright but I swear the shadow on that coffee shop be growing every day swear that shit be gettin darker with each sunrise saw it stretch over some niggas on Livingston and when it went away they was just gone like they got swallowed by some other kind of black niggas ain't drinkin coffee niggas don't need to be any more awake niggas seen too much death to sleep I ain't slept since they tore down the school and built a new graveyard I ain't slept since my son got that toy gun for Christmas but my hands still steady I still got my name on this door my girl said the hood gonna be alright

SHERIDAN AVENUE, 2002

Ain't no Uzis made in Harlem. Not one of us in here owns a poppy field. This thing is bigger than Me. This is big business. This is the American way.

Nino Brown

Blessed

be that which blooms from the hand of an unruly child and unravels in the spring air to make its way back to that which birthed it. the home,

both this one in front of us, and all of the other towering kingdoms on this land which is not truly ours, but still feels like it is ours by right, or by the journey

of our ancestors. the april night and the arrogance it pours over our bones. the first reminder of warmth. blessed be the bathroom stalls in saylor-ackermann hall, and those inside

of them tonight, digging for the toilet paper that will not be found there, but instead will be found suspended along the tree branches outside of these homes
our college majors will never allow us to afford

blessed be the repurposing of these everyday tools. how it was perhaps learned from our grandmothers who learned from their

grandmothers. how a rubber band could also tie back the untamed hair. how the potatoes and milk could become a meal. how so many things could be used
to whip,

to force the skin open and risen like a loaf of cornbread. how that which cleans us can also cause such chaos when it mixes with the anger built into the one black

44

boy in every class, the one black boy on the soccer team, the one black boy at the cafeteria table, the lighthouse in a still ocean

blessed be the trees, and all things hanging

from them. the wind, and how it tastes faintly of salt and sweat after it catches our 2-ply revolution and calls the lowest hanging remnants to dance until the ends of the toilet paper resemble violently twitching

legs, and everyone keeps laughing but I look away, only for a moment, to remind myself of the trees and how many bodies they have claimed

and still claim. how they do not ask for forgiveness, and therefore have earned this reckoning. blessed be the ghetto.

the one six blocks east, where the foundations of churches lean to match the wasting bodies of those inside. where I am convinced my father is watching this exact moment over prayer beads and mumbling *I ain't paying no 25,000 dollars a year for this shit.* where the gunshots became late

night spirituals, rocking entire blocks to sleep. and where the police no longer come, though it is silent right now and there are whole families alive in these houses, and the sidewalks are even and this is how I remember that we are not in the ghetto

tonight, even before the sirens. even before the blue and red lights, and how they consume everything in the dark and guide us home, the way light used to when "home" was another state, or another country. blessed be this blending of running and laughter. a language known since the abandonment of crawling.

this time bomb of youth which explodes in an alley behind Johnson's Bar and paints the walls. these shoes that carried us, mine pure, and white as the weapons we chose this evening. mine, too expensive for my work study job. mine, the reason I borrow

Stephanie's books for our women's studies class. mine, a home on an even sidewalk with whole families alive inside. blessed be the crack of a good can when it opens. the empty case of natural light on a dorm room floor, and how the contents of that case once combined

with the bed of flaming hot Cheetos lining inexperienced stomachs. the burn of rejection. that which dances down our throats and then claws its way out screaming, the friend next to me right now who cannot take this truth, and the heaving that follows, and the thick river of orange-red that follows that, directly on top of my shoes, white mere seconds ago, but now a mural of the setting sun, beyond saving.

Blessed

be the destruction of all things too beautiful to endure an untouched life. until God gets even.

SAYLOR-ACKERMANN HALL, 2004

My white friend Chad lets the word *nigga* spill and
paint the dorm room a whole new shade
of trouble but I know he doesn't mean it the same way
police on Sheridan Avenue mean it when they ask
why I'm *dressed that way* in *this part of town* while I fumble
for my college ID so that I might be spared the handcuffs
                this time
or a few less grass stains on the one good
pair of pants I own;
anyway I know Chad doesn't understand how a word can
hang in the air and multiply twice its weight before it ever
comes down I guess because we slapped
hands and hugged tight like brothers in the hallway
just ten minutes ago or maybe because Biggie died on this night
back in '97 and we mourn loud enough
for a room full of white kids to rap
every word without the slightest blush like when Biggie says
niggas bleed just like us and I watch the air get thick above
my head and become an anvil.

47

I MEAN MAYBE NONE OF US ARE ACTUALLY FROM ANYWHERE

it's so hard to trace these things right
I just rolled out of bed one morning and
I had this head of good hair and when I say
good hair I mean it was passed down from someone
who was once dragged through a field by it until
their scalp became a wide open mouth but it looks fly
tucked underneath this fitted hat on the dance floor no
you cannot borrow this dance you cannot stand over
another dark and shaking body and breathe in the
smoke we leave in our wake I get that we are all
human or whatever but I don't even
know what that would do to your bones I don't know if
your bones bend like mine I come from a boxed in
culture I come from people who traveled entire oceans
wrapped around each other I was born from a woman
who is now inside a box so you see some things are
just natural for me you're right maybe there is no such
thing as a country
maybe there is just gutted land and rows of sharp
teeth that have torn at my flesh for so long I'm not
exactly sure which wound is the one I belong to I mean
the only way I recognize my skin is when it is

open

       and spilling how can I even keep track you know it must be
       nice to wrap your hands around an unscarred body it must
       be nice to wrap your tongue around all of the words in that
       song without also asking to bleed out on a sidewalk look all
       I know is

       I began running when the fire started and I haven't stopped
       since maybe I come from running maybe running is a
       country maybe everyone who lives there misses someone
       they thought would live forever

I'm glad you don't know how to find it I'm glad
that you haven't caught me yet I'm glad you have a
black friend I'm sorry
that your black friend may die soon
and then there will only be me

OK, I'M FINALLY READY TO SAY I'M SORRY FOR THAT ONE SUMMER

when I watched *American Pie 2* twice a week & listened to all nine minutes of "Konstantine" on the way to every party with the sun still out in a car thick with sober voices spilling out of the windows & making another mess all over the sidewalks. I guess this is what it looks like when youth is writhing on its deathbed but the boys who claim it are still very much alive & blooming & being split in half by a beam of moonlight stumbling in through a window and falling all over the sheets in a bed that is not ours. In the heat of that summer, I escaped the parties on Friday nights to find the near-silent bedroom of a girl who I pretended to stop talking to when my friends said we're college guys now, but who I used to shoot hoops with in the backyard & skipped out on prom to go record shopping with last spring & that summer, we would sit on her floor & let the Supremes record play all the way through twice & tell each other stories about how our college roommates snored all year & how we didn't sleep like we used to under this city's moon & how we never got used to eating alone & how we instead got used to hunger & how small we've become because of all these things & then we would lay with each other without ever touching & I didn't know how to talk about distance out loud & in the mornings over breakfast with the guys when Jeff would yell how was it last night across the table & I knew what it carried even then & I still smiled into a brown tornado of coffee until the plates rattled with fists pounding & laughter & high fives & isn't it funny how silence can undress two bodies & press them into each other? & when I say funny I mean the feeling that stretches itself out in your stomach while you watch someone cry into their palms & turn their face to the night before they walk away from you for what you know is the last time before there is new sharp & boundless city between the both of you forever & when fall came, boys sat up in their beds alone & gasping while their hearts rattled out the ghosts of every unspoken love that dragged them there & then a whole country crawled itself across the ocean & went to war.

ODE TO PETE WENTZ, ENDING IN TYLER'S FUNERAL

There is already more than enough blood in your city tonight and yet I know you are at the edge of another tower of speakers, stacked higher than the dead boys pulled from the southside and forgotten. To jump knowing you will be caught is a type of mercy I have never known, yet craved. You can love a whole scene until it becomes a flooded house, and then I suppose climbing is the only option. Still, we wore all black every summer like the sun didn't snarl. Didn't have teeth, never wanted to tear into our skin and let the salt of us pour out in waves, or like our skin wasn't suspect enough before we decided to be rebels. Before we walked into corner stores with no money and walked out with chocolate melting against the warmth of our thighs. We wrote *"IGNORE YOUR GOD COMPLEX"* in every bathroom stall on campus one of those years even though we knew the right lyrics, because on a night we were too poor to afford concert tickets we pressed our backs into a hill overlooking the LC, and the way Patrick's voice swung into the air when singing *"Loaded God Complex"*, we couldn't tell the difference, just knew we discovered a message that had to be delivered on the walls of places where people emptied themselves of everything they challenged their insides to own. In those days, we were drunk on reaching up and pulling the night sky apart, swallowing it in chunks, until we were as dark inside as we were out. Until it held us tight like no one else dared to. We boys and our misery, Pete. I know you fumble over your instrument. I know your trembling hands approach the strings like a virgin lover, reaching to pull fabric from the edge of the first person to whisper their desires in an ear, but if not for the bass, how else would you fall into our outstretched arms? Who else would we have to drag us home by the collars with the windows down on 270 after another set of hours in a Midwest that is not like the one in your songs, but if we turn up the music loud enough we can pretend they aren't breaking our old neighborhoods into swarms of dust? We can pretend there aren't boys running out of scattered glass temples, with their hands raised, begging for someone to open their chests, the heat

51

unthawing whatever happiness they have left. And I know these are just my problems, I know there is blood in your city that craves the rush of a cold sidewalk every night, that there are so many ways to stop a city from breathing all at once, to twist it into something sharp and metal and turn it in on itself, and you can't possibly fit another tragedy in a song after all these years, can you? Not even for one of us who fell so in love with his own loneliness that it became a flooded house and he climbed like you did to the edge of a rooftop with wet shoes and jumped because Pete, when you were lonely and you jumped, we sang and held you up to the roof and you survived another night, and then another year, and you gave a boy a name that we laughed at, and we did not have to bury you underneath a split tree in Columbus. But we still wore black then and every summer after, we still stole candy bars and planted them on a hill outside the LC and prayed for them to melt this time into the ghosts of everyone we had ever loved, and would never see again. Then we lost so many friends that we truly became criminals, and rummaged through this splintered city to find god because a man outside of a bar convinced us all of our friends were in heaven and none of us knew any other way to get there saddled by all of these sins and all of this sadness. Until one night, drunk off the sky again, we figured maybe we can all get to heaven if we ignore our god complex. Maybe if we stack all of the speakers in this town as high as we can and begin to go up, we can escape even this.

ON MELTING

I am still fascinated by the glint of warm
light that echoes off the snow and arrives to throw a small blanket

on the uncovered flesh of anyone brave
enough to walk through another harsh winter

even after decades encased in the Midwest during such loveless
hours when the streets become covered in white like

everywhere we look is another anchored ghost clawing at the
window but this is the season where I will make the face

of a girl on a cookie and pass it to her across a room full of
strangers which is a weird way to say

I think I could love you until even the sun grows tired
of coming back every

spring to forgive us for another season of hiding
but it is not like me to be brave

at least not until there is enough warmth for the corner to flood
again with this city's melting

until the boys tear their hands from the cold glass and
burst fearless again into the wetness

especially not when I can miss a stranger who may not remember
me for months, or fill a notebook with

questions I might ask from across a table in the soft buzz
of a coffee shop while two drinks grow cold

yet still not as cold as the night we first laughed at the
same joke or at least

the first time her laugh drifted across a room and
I hungered for better humor

before I walked home in three sweaters and two pairs
of pants, shivering in the darkness

asking myself how long it would be before I could finally
peel back all of those layers and become a

new, unbreakable device

†††.

Loneliness comes with life.

Whitney Houston

THE MUSIC OR THE MISERY

I do not mean the cartoon heart. the one that swells from the wolf's chest. when distracted by a girl wolf. his tongue rolling onto the hot pavement. right before the anvil drops from an impossible height. and he is crushed again. foiled by a man's hunger. I say "heart" and mean the actual heart. I saw my heart in the eyes of my mother. it was too small to save her. I wrote my heart in a poem. it took up the whole bedroom. it doesn't pay rent. it stays up watching cities   burn to the ground. I am so sorry that you have nowhere to sit. I just loved someone yesterday.   so you see the dilemma. I just promised someone that I would watch them grow old in a country that wants them dead. so I just can't spare any more room.   here. take this mixtape I made. it is just 30 minutes of the wind. how it sounds when being cut by something heavy. falling from the sky. making an endlessly dark shadow at my feet. while I blow a kiss.

THE AUTHOR EXPLAINS GOOD KID, M.A.A.D. CITY TO HIS WHITE FRIEND WHILE DRIVING THROUGH SOUTHEAST OHIO

"…and anyway, we ain't all grow up the SAME kinda poor.
I know them country boys out here wanna act like the blunt be
some vice for the uncivilized but don't we all feel better settin' fire
to some shit when we with the homies? ain't that how so many
white crosses made the fields dry and empty after the black
families moved too close to town? God knows I be of a
complexion responsible for so many empty harvests. so many
hungry daughters, and we still don't know what to do with all
this violence but put one of them big gold frames around it and
pray it might sell a million copies or somethin' so our mothers
can get up out them homes with the leaning bricks, that is if they
still breathing. don't nobody out here know what that is. fields
out here might just need a good song, 'least that's what the end of
a good whip used to whisper into the backs of my great-great-
great ancestors. last week, heard your moms say the dairy queen
off route 36 was "ghetto" and I figured that meant it been
sandwiched between a juke that only played Sam Cooke and a
grandmotherly sort who never stops swaying when the wind calls,
just trynna stay alive since she don't know what's next cuz she
stopped believing in heaven when all her children caught them
bullets for wearing red or blue or the night on their skin, but it
turns out the dairy queen was just out of vanilla soft serve. the
men out in the fields here be letting the sun cook their skin bright
pink, chewin' on those big cigars like "why can't they just get
back to the good old days when a fistfight could solve it all?" but
trayvon and jordan and 'em still dead, and we still only know
the way to fill something empty be with these songs or some other
shit loud and covered in smoke"

DISPATCHES FROM THE BLACK BARBERSHOP, TONY'S CHAIR. 2011.

shit ain't nobody out here gonna care bout you bein lonely out in them suburbs like your pops ain't still right down the street nigga like you ain't already home but the hood ain't what it used to be you see they got a fancy ice cream shop where the corner store was they got a sports bar where the record store was and what we supposed to do for records where we supposed to go for that old school shit how we supposed to heal see that's why these new lil niggas only listen to the radio that's why ain't no love songs played at the block party no more that's why niggas fight all summer long swear every time a black boy throw a punch the city be puttin up another strip mall where we used to dance light-skinned jeff got knocked out on east main by a sucker punch that broke up the 4th of july cookout in front of brenda's hair shop and when he woke up it was a whole foods see that's why you sittin up here talkin bout you lonely while my rent goin up every month but I still got my name on the door I ain't listenin to that new rap them boys bring in here shit sound too wild for me I gotta get behind your ear real quick yeah my son be driving around in my car listenin to that shit got the whole car shaking got the whole hood shaking got bricks falling right out of buildings and turning to dust got whole houses collapsing swear the church was still there three Sundays ago a nigga ain't prayed to god in three weeks my girl says I got to get right says ain't none of us too far off from heaven nigga god don't care if you lonely ain't nobody more lonely than god you know god ain't got no friends all god got is questions all god got is one million hands lookin for grace ain't nothing more lonely than watchin everything you built collapse ain't nothing more lonely than watching a whole block swallowed by smoke nigga ain't nothing more lonely than having the power to put out a fire and not making it rain

61

AT THE HOUSE PARTY WHERE WE FOUND OUT WHITNEY HOUSTON WAS DEAD

I am tucked in the corner,
underneath a choir of arching floorboards
wailing for sympathy from about four dozen relentless feet,
and I am telling Jasmine that there is like,
ONE song that everyone at this party knows all of the words to.
I tell her that we were all born of the 80s.
All born of parents who watched the revolution
shove itself into a too small suit at the turn of a decade that
left them in homes with welcome mats that read:
"Your hearts are the lost luggage at the airport of the next generation."
I tell her because of this
we have earned one song we all know the words to,
in the same way we have earned this breeze,
sitting on top of our skin tonight and staying,
the way any good apology does
while we scroll through our iPods shouting out 80s pop songs
we both kind of love like a secret,
and we keep scrolling right up until
someone runs into this room that is over capacity
by at least nine righteous, glowing bodies
and tells us that Whitney Houston woke up dead
in Los Angeles two hours ago.
Our friend Amber is like five PBRs deep,
and drunk enough to yell at her boyfriend
for the Whitney Houston-less iPod he has been using
to DJ this party.

We, the war generation.
The only way we know how to bury our dead
is with blood, or sweat, or sex
or anything pouring from wet skin

to signify we were here, and the wooden floor
of a basement belonging to an old house on Neil Avenue
makes as good a burial ground as any,
says the small boom box now playing DJ
in the center of this room,
and the Whitney CD inside,
pouring out of the speakers just loudly enough
to let everyone in this room
get a small taste of Whitney alive and young,
and telling us exactly how to squeeze exactly what we are owed
out of this Saturday night
when I don't understand where love lives
in the way I will understand where love lives in coming months,
but I understand there is a saxophone solo
at about 3 minutes and 30 seconds
into the song "How Will I Know",
and I'm pretty sure love has a vacation home there,
and we are all invited tonight when steam rises off of these bodies
like a sacrifice and the first time I see Jasmine cry
is when we are watching all of our friends
convert grief into perspiration. I tell her that I see our reflection
in the pools of sweat, and we look like two flowers
that have never stopped opening, I say,
We be bloomed so wide by the end of this night
won't nothing in this city be able to hold us

later, we press our backs into the roof of a house that even at 4am
sways with us like a metronome of well-timed memorial. The sky
is unchained, and careless, and wrapped around us both
like our long discarded childhoods.
I look up and ask myself again why the stars have so long tolerated
the audacity of clouds. I laugh loudly and tell Jasmine that
it is
impossible for a human being to wake up dead.
She is already asleep.

THE GHOST OF THE AUTHOR'S MOTHER HAS A CONVERSATION WITH HIS FIANCEE ABOUT HIGHWAYS

...and down south, honey. When the side of the road began to swell with dead and dying things, that's when us black children knew it was summer. Daddy didn't keep clocks in the house. Ain't no use when the sky round those parts always had some flames runnin' to horizon, lookin' like the sun was always out. back when I was a little girl, I swear, them white folk down south would do anything to stop another dark thing from touching the land, even the nighttime. We ain't have streetlights, or some grandmotherly voice riding through the fields on horseback tellin' us when to come inside. What we had was the stomach of a deer, split open on route 59. What we had was flies resting on the exposed insides of animals with their tongues touching the pavement. What we had was the smell of gunpowder and the promise of more to come, and, child, that'll get you home before the old folks would break out the moonshine and celebrate another day they didn't have to pull the body of someone they loved from the river. I say "river" because I want you to always be able to look at the trees without crying. When we moved east, I learned how a night sky can cup a black girl in its hands and ask for forgiveness. My daddy sold the pistol he kept in the sock drawer and took me to the park. Those days, I used to ask him what he feared, and he always said "the bottom of a good glass." And then he stopped answering. And then he stopped coming home altogether.

Something about the first day of a season, honey. Something always gotta sacrifice its blood. Everything that has its time must be lifted from the earth. My boys don't bother with seasons anymore. My sons went to sleep in the spring once and woke up to a motherless summer. All they know now is that it always be colder than it should be. I wish I could fix this for you. I'm sorry none of my children wear suits anymore. I wish ties didn't remind my boys of shovels, and dirt, and an empty living room. They all used to look so nice in ties. I'm sorry that you may come home one day to the smell of rotting meat, every calendar you own torn off the walls, burning in a trashcan.
And it will be the end of spring.
And you will know.

MY WIFE SAYS THAT IF YOU LIVE 20 YEARS

Without having to go to a funeral, you are really lucky. The girl on TV is no older than I was when everyone in my quivering home learned to hustle one more ghost into our already overflowing pockets & even though it is not real, she is being swallowed by a carnivorous grief that is howling & escaping through the screen on all fours, pacing around at our feet & begging us to move. Pissing on the blanket sewed by a grandmother's hands. Hands that were once a salve for every wound, hands that once clapped along with the good gospel in a church shack & once cupped a child's crying face & once broke bread & then one day just broke. Outside, another sky undresses itself to its blood-red flesh & what kind of world is this to bring a child into anyway? The names we carry have been carved into so much stone clutching the ground in Ohio it is impossible to consider how many years it would take to lift them out and pass them on to anyone as small as the crumbs from a good meal. but who are we to deny our families the delivery of new blood? New hands to assist with the burial and becoming of the earth that chews at the edges of whatever years our elders have left & maybe even us in our youth even though we moved out the hood & gunshots don't echo over the river out here & boys don't leave the barren fields & go to war just so they can fall asleep with full stomachs. It is somehow easy to forget that there are so many ways to die while black & not all of them involve being made hollow while the world watches & isn't that a funny thing? How there is all this danger I ignore & make plans for 2016 & beyond

& beyond & our fathers still want grandchildren in spite of all this & I am afraid that if I do not raise children to carry the heft of me when I die, I will be only bones after my soul exits to spare all of you such heavy lifting & how awful would that be & who would speak of me around a drunk & buzzing table when the card game runs dry? on the elevator, when the woman eyes how I lock fingers with my wife, she leans in close & tells us she can tell we're newlyweds & we smile & she asks how many children we're going to have & I look past her face & into the metal wall where my fading reflection is whispering *enough to carry endless caskets through the sinking mud.*

XII

No one
wants to be the person
who drives slow past a flower shop
on valentine's day
while their lover sleeps
even if I know the flower petals
will fold in on themselves
and turn to rust
before they expand
into the sun
beautiful things die
every day and we
still stare while they
are living or set them
in the middle of a
wooden table passed
down from a wilting
grandmother who only
remembers your face
on tuesdays
it makes sense to
declare love with
something that makes no promises
about how long it will stay living
something that we know
will be dead in a week
I tell myself that
while gently pressing my
fingers into the dark
leather of another pair of sneakers
while all of the other men
scramble for chocolate
I try on another beautiful thing that
may live to see me
forgiven for walking
through the door

holding it close to
my chest
nothing else in my hands
I understand that I should
always come
bearing flowers
it is good to hold
a slow funeral
in your palms
it is good to know
when something
will leave

MY WIFE SAYS THAT EVERYONE OUR AGE RIGHT NOW IS LISTENING

To NPR & I suspect this is why we had to spend so much money
on alcohol for the wedding
I mean don't get me wrong
on a depleted highway in Ohio licked clean
of light we all do what we have to do to survive but I don't
think anyone has ever unzipped a Saturday night in a
buzzing city by getting low to
A Prairie Home Companion
then again it's not like I know how to party really
I told myself I could never drink alcohol when I was 18 after
we dared Chris to drink seven beers in an alley &
he tumbled his limbs into a tameless dance on College Avenue
before stumbling into an oncoming #2 bus & ever since
that afternoon he only listens to talk radio &
so the least I can do is buy you this beer &
by "you" I mean anyone who can still feel things below their
waist in a bar with an endless jukebox
it is so easy to leap into someone else's skin
& wear it when the bass floods a room & so
why is everyone I love so immovable
maybe we should try and invent new dances because
I can't do any of the ones I see on TV anymore I think
my dance will be mostly arms
& the rest of me will look like it is sinking or
fighting against some other violent thing
that will inevitably swallow me whole
another burning city or
another sleepless night in America
& maybe this dance will catch on & then
no one will even notice how all of this joyous screaming bends
itself into tears.

THE GHOST OF THE AUTHOR'S MOTHER TEACHES HIS WIFE HOW TO COOK FRIED CHICKEN

...And child, when you take skin swollen and damp from the river and the blood, and you throw it in the heat, everything pops. You gotta cover your eyes, baby. Hold them children close. My mama's mama said that's how God made the south. Said there was nothing but grass and then, one day, all this wet black skin. Said it popped so loud when they set them down in the blazing stomach of the new world, them plantation fields split clean open and then there was cotton. And then idle hands for the picking, and then war, and after that, we all woke up with our skin covered in hot grease, birds following us everywhere and so at least we was eating good.

Wasn't nothing to do back then but tear into the flesh of something you own. Swallow something you raised before the rest of the world took hold of it. Now, child, it don't matter how dark the body is. That ain't how you tell when something is done. When it's limp and floating, you gotta take something sharp to the heart of it. It's ready to be taken if it ain't got no more blood to give. That's how them white boys from Birmingham knew they done got granddaddy good. Left him in the dirt road we walked to school, flesh burned from the cross and bloated from the drowning.

That's when mama moved us to where the black men ain't know the first thing 'bout cooking. 'bout giving themselves over for a meal. I been in kitchens my whole life, girl. You drop enough things into a burning place, you learn all kinda new prayers. Learn just how to cover them eyes. When to get them babies away from the heat.

My youngest boy don't know no better. He ain't never seen the broken remains of a man melting into the asphalt so he be reaching his hands too far into the flames. Used to bring me food still dripping in oil. Soaked through the plate. Got buried with the scent of it still dancing on my fingertips. Thought if I just swallowed enough of my child's food, the world would keep him safe. If I could take this full belly into heaven might hold me over 'til I could touch his face again. 'Til he loved another woman enough to cook for her. 'Til another woman loved him enough to rip every stove out of the wall.

MY WIFE SAYS THAT THERE ARE SO MANY SONGS

That aren't about what we thought they were when we were kids. There hasn't been anything romantic written since the 70s. All songs are about how much of someone we can take into ourselves until we both become dust. It is evening once more. By the time we go to sleep there will be another city to call our own. Another home to fold us into its cracked hands. I pick branches off of my mother's grave again. I don't know what will stretch itself over the stone after I have left it to its own growing. Everyone tells me that the Third Eye Blind song isn't about what I thought it was about in 1997 when we covered the head of the cold body. When the men carried the coffin and buried it here. I walked the streets of a borrowed city with headphones and stopped speaking. Only allowed my mouth to shape itself around the words of this dirge that spilled out of pop radio, out of college house parties. And tonight, as the state where we fell in love becomes another ghost between us, playing a mixtape I made, it leaps out the speakers. I sing along to the line *I'm smiling, she's living; she's golden* and then rewind it.

NOTES ON WAITING FOR THE DOG TO FIND THE PERFECT PLACE TO TAKE A SHIT WHILE MORNING CUTS THROUGH THE SKY, FRESH FROM ANOTHER DARKNESS

perhaps on the crest of each stiff blade of grass hangs the
eternal name of someone who was once loved but is now
vanished and just another
name in an endless field
of names that is newly remembered with
each return trip of the eager nose,
the trampling paws creating a frantic circle in
the soft ground
in preparation for this most naked moment the
romance is always in the ritual
before the ritual
how I pace flat rings into the carpet
on the days my wife is gone long enough
for her name to grow beneath my feet
and stretch up the walls while
sunlight takes its final drinks from a
cracked-open skyline
but I know the words for this
for what it is to leave and eventually return to
the space in a bed
that is yours and yours alone
even after a lover has starved
themselves with distance how
exhausting it must be to come
back to this stretch of
grass each morning with no language to
speak an apology for your absence
what it must be like to have nothing to give
of yourself but what has been consumed and then
passed through you

a gift to show that you can still
hold things
That you are not yet
ready for burial.

THE AUTHOR WRITES THE FIRST
DRAFT OF HIS WEDDING VOWS

(An erasure of Virginia Woolf's suicide letter to her husband, Leonard)

Dearest,

I feel certain I am going mad again.

we will go through   terrible times. And   recover . I
begin to hear your voice, and can't   concentrate. So I am
doing what seems

will give me the greatest possible happiness.

I don't think two people could   have been happier   with
this disease. I know
that without   you   I can't properly feel .

What I want to say is You   have

saved me.

Everything has gone from me

but the certainty of your goodness.

ON SAINTHOOD

Used to be,

when one of our own was made ready for heaven, before the bull-necked men were sent off with their shovels to heave whatever dirt they needed to make a dark bed for the bloodless, someone's child filled their cheeks with newly precious air and blew a horn. Someone's daddy, even weary of this scene, pressed his hands to a drum. The mothers threw back their heads and found some

song, restless to fight its way out of their grief-drowned lungs. Something slow to clamber up the clouds and let God know they weren't done praying yet, even as his house overflowed with husbands, or wives, or sweet sons and daughters who never got to watch their name waltz along a lover's lips for the first time. And then, there would be another horn. Another drum. More joyous clatter and sweat-licked skin pressed close together, singing out the same gospel.

And eventually,

someone in a suit too loud for such dark ceremonies would break out into a dance, spilling themselves onto the pavement while a hearse rolled slow enough to keep time with the beat the bodies gathering in a holy sway, a two-step kissed with despair, one hundred black hips pulled towards the sky, two hundred black hands grasping for the tips of every ropeless tree

and then the street would become its own country

and then the sweat was a cool river that the babies pushed their cupped palms into, discovering thirst

and anyone who ever woke up from a dream where they were making love to a ghost got out of their cars and danced

and anyone standing by a cracked window for whole years, waiting
for their child to walk through a door, ran from their homes
and sang

and the ground would shake for miles with
the skyline, bending down to give shade where there was none
before

and everyone put a hand on the casket, even if the person inside
did not share their blood, but did give the reason for the clap
and holler or

the sweetness of a long goodbye for anyone
who had made a room of their emptiness
and longed to fill it with another celebration
stretching itself into a ripe and hot night

Yes,

it truly must take nothing but grief to turn our people into a choir.
I know the way a song can turn up in a mouth when the wind
blows another city's burning into our own. A boy bleeds
in the street for four hours and I hum
a song I do not know
in the shower with my grandmother's voice.
My mouth widens with each black body left
for dead.

But,

there is still no dance today for the rage that grows over
your own skin and builds an unshakeable home.
Or, at least no dance that
doesn't look like dying can look when it sets upon someone
who wishes to live.

The man pleads *enough*
while we watch an arm fasten itself to his neck and squeeze out
what breath he has left.
His thick and heavy limbs twitch
against their own leaving
The legs jerk, the hips thrust towards the
clouds in offering again like hips used to
when the clouds were still interested in such
sacrifice.

And,

as the man finally gives in, I call
out to God.

A horn cuts across the sky.

IV.

GRACE: *You know, we all hear about all the stages of grieving that you`re supposed to go through to get healthy again. I don`t know how you can do that when you wake up every morning and relive the whole thing. How -- when you first wake up in the morning, Ms. McSpadden, before your feet hit the floor, what`s your first thought?*

MCSPADDEN: *I don`t even know. To be honest with you, I don`t even know. I can`t even tell you my thought process since August 9th. My mind is just all over the place.*

GRACE: *Mr. Brown, I remember I would wake up and I would think everything had been a horrible, horrible dream, and then it didn`t take me long to remember it was real, and that is how my day would start. And that lasted for years. When you first get up in the morning, what hits you? What`s the first thing?*

BROWN: *That I`m not going to see my son again. It`s hard to even close my eyes -- flashes and pictures. It`s just -- it`s hard. During the time when I`m asleep, I don`t even know I`m asleep. I just wake up, like, Wow, I`m asleep, you know, because it`s so hard to just -- I close my eyes,*

that`s all I see.

From the transcript of a CNN interview between
Nancy Grace and the parents of Michael Brown

I DO NOT CALL THIS "WAR"

I do not stand in the doorway and kiss my wife like I will never see
     her again
I do not say *noose* when I mean *bullet*
I do not say *bullet* when I am asked what keeps me awake at night
I do not keep track of the names
I do not keep track of my own body
I do not look at graves
I do not look at televisions
I do not look in the eyes of the interviewer
when he asks how there can be *so much violence* in my poems
I do not look honest enough to survive

I have maybe left my home
for the last time

MY WIFE SAYS THAT IT'S A GOOD THING HUMANS DON'T HOLD FEAR

in their skin the way dogs do
which I guess is easy to say while driving at
night through a neighborhood where the houses got
more rooms than the bodies inside them could
ever fill even after they have chewed the skin off of
another old black church & built a shopping
mall over its bones
but on the eastside of Columbus the
police ain't been around since that new
year's party where I learned
that you can tell the difference between
gunshots & fireworks by how fast your
mama pulls you back from the window
& begins to say another one of those
hushed prayers & on the eastside of Columbus
them boys flash headlights twice on
saturday nights to let the
women know to get the babies inside cuz
another one of the homies bled out behind
greenbrier on friday & now someone else's son ain't
gonna make it to church in the morning
& maybe their younger brothers will praise
the empty space in the bed
after all of the mourning has
peeled itself off of the project walls
& maybe boys will begin to
praise the bigger portions served
at the dinner table after
a brother leaves & never returns
we from the hood after all
so maybe distance is a currency
when boys pile themselves on top
of their families & that is how a bed is

made for the night
it must be nice to have enough rooms
in a home to store things
so that you never have to make a rupture
of your own stomach & fill it with
all of the times you could have been
dragged through the glass-ridden
street choking on the memory of
someone who could maybe save
you but will never come & there are
so many moments like these writhing
under the skin of black boys
you would think that we would
always be full & never hunger
for anything
& yet

ODE TO JAY-Z, ENDING IN THE RATTLE OF A FIEND'S TEETH

teach us how to hustle so / hard that they / never come for our daughters and / feast upon their dancing limbs or / the thick tangles of hair swarming / over their dark eyes / have we prayed at your feet / long enough for them to keep / what they came here with / after they are entombed in / the dirt / this is what is happening / in our America right now / another black girl was emptied / in Brooklyn last night and / I watch this on the news / in Ohio and weep / even though I know that it is not / my mother / because the girl on TV has / no name other than *gone* / and my mother held on / to her name until her body / became ash / until she was a mountain of white / powder / that's that shit / we take razor blades to / and drown / the whole hood in / that shit that got us out / the projects / and left whole families / of men starved and longing / is this what becomes / of the women we love / consumed even in death by / a flock of men / who have mistaken their grief / for a persistent hunger / that comes again each / sweat-soaked morning with / a new set of freshly forgotten corpses / overflowing in its arms / after coming down from / the cross / how did you fix your hands / to hold a child without / covering her in decades / of blood / and have you taught her / to run yet / not the way we run / into the arms of a lover / but the way you ran / before the first gold record hung / in a home far enough away / from the block / you finally stopped / hearing the clatter of ravening jaws / clashing together at sunset / we still hear it out here / it gets louder with each / black girl hollowed out / and erased / if you can't feed them into silence / again / can you at least rap for us / over all this noise / everyone I love has had / the hardest time / sleeping

WHILE WATCHING THE CONVENIENCE STORE BURN IN BALTIMORE, POETS ON THE INTERNET ARGUE OVER ANOTHER ARTICLE DECLARING "POETRY IS DEAD"

I mean is it dead really did we watch its mother pull its limp carcass from the mouth of a night that it walked into living are there one hundred black hands carrying its casket through the boulevard did it die in a city that no one thought about until it was burning did broken glass rain onto the streets in its memory did people weep at the shatter did people cry for the convenience store and forget the corpse did the reek of rising gas drain the white from a child's eyes did we stop speaking its good dead name when a fist was thrown do we even remember what killed it anymore I think it was split at its spine but I can't recall I just woke up one day with this new empty can we uproot the corpse and drag it through the streets will people remember if we lay it at the boots of those who last saw it alive are we calling it dead because white people got bored with its living who will be left to bend the night into a chorus how will we harvest skin to pull tight over a wooden face who is going to ready the drum

USAvCUBA

after Frank O'Hara

It is 3:15 on a Saturday & I am in a car on I-95 on the way to the soccer game & Nate is riding shotgun which is also the name for when you plunge something sharp into a can of beer & split open its aluminum shell before swallowing its urgent sacrifice & I once saw Nate do this five times in one night before the Mount Union game & we got to the field late the next morning smelling like something coughed up in the heat of a 1980s summer & it was almost as hot then as it is right now in this traffic that isn't moving & hasn't moved for what feels like thirty years which is to say that it feels like we haven't moved since we were too small to speak & burden everyone we love with our refusal to crawl back into silence & every car on this highway is in park & somehow people are still pressing on their horns & Nate turns up the radio & David Ruffin is singing *I wish it would rain* & his voice is unfolding long & slow in the backseat like an eager lover & there is a whole history of men demanding the sky to shake at their command & I'm not saying out loud whether or not I believe in god & I'm not saying out loud what I know the rain means I'm only saying that I need this dry summer to stay dry I'm only saying that the tickets to this game cost as much as my best suit & kickoff is at 3:30 & we are absolutely going to be late & there is a whole history of black people being late to things & there is a whole language signaling our arrival & there is an entire catalog of jokes that dissect this happening & they never get old & by *they* I mean *black people in America* & I can hear the joke our college soccer coach made when the only two black boys on the team stumbled late onto a hot field & lateness always makes for a good joke

the punchline is I slept through my mother's final breaths or the punchline is I stumbled into a living room thick with a family's grief while clearing a night's salt from my eyes or the punchline is that I'm always running late I'm always running I'm always trying to move time backwards & tell everyone that I love them & isn't that funny & Nate points to an ambulance speeding down the highway opposite us & disappearing into the sun & I don't want to think that there might be a body inside of it & then all of the cars start moving

AFTER THE CAMERAS LEAVE, IN THREE PARTS

I. The Ghost Of The Author's Mother Performs An Autopsy On The Freshly Hollow City

They listenin' to the wrong music again, child. When the smoke rises and sinks its teeth into the meat of another dark sky, people always wanna act like "Mississippi Goddam" was the only song Nina Simone blessed the earth with. Probably 'cuz if you sit on the floor with a record player in a room quiet as a dirt-lined casket, you can hear the black bones cracking right there underneath the piano keys. You can taste another man's blood climbing slow up the back of your throat. Feel the water cannons start to press through the walls and soak your feet. Might even be able to see the one hundred snapped necks hanging from the edge of the needle when Nina sings "Lord have mercy on this land of mine..."

And if that don't carry you to the front lines of any city trynna paint its streets with your blood, lord knows nothin' will.

But didn't nobody sing "Sinnerman" like Nina. Didn't no one else cast that spell right. The confessional ain't no good if nobody confessin'. Nina, though. Let every note of "Sinnerman" hunt for a wicked tongue. Forced it to lift its secrets to the warm air. You play that song over what's left of any scorched city, and watch. All them white men gonna start runnin' from they homes, crying what haunts them into their bloody palms. 'Til the middle of the street splits wide open. Swallows them whole. I know. It ain't gonna bring nobody's dead child back. But I ain't seen "Mississippi Goddam" do nothin' 'cept flood a house of black bodies 'til they washed up in the heat of a city, bloated and dying.

My daddy never taught me to swim.
I ain't never take my babies to the water.

II.   The Convenience Store's Broken Glass Speaks

have they stopped / whispering the dead thing's name yet? / I was promised / the brick's heavy kiss / would spread me thin / over where they killed the boy / and then I would become the new / dead thing / to grow ripe in every mouth / I would become the thing they remember / in the summer / I show up to the party late / and loud / I drink the house into a desert / I keep the whole world thirsty / I stay after everyone else leaves / I keep you awake until the sun comes / I crumble the body / I leave the jagged void / I part the whole country / I Moses the Midwest / come children / walk through my toothed bed / to the other shore / we don't talk about death over here / we don't speak its name / we don't speak of leaving / we wake up to a new day / we don't think of who didn't / look at me here / stretched out on this holy ground / like I'm almost human / like I'm almost worth grieving / and why not? / people have to mourn the shatter / of anything that they can / look into / and see how alive / they still are

III.   What Is Left Of "Sinnerman", After The Fire

Oh,

      sinner

          run

sinner   run

run

        Don't you see

this

        bleedin' river

        Don't you see   the devil

              waitin'

DISPATCHES FROM THE BLACK BARBERSHOP, TONY'S CHAIR. 2015.

and I got to walk my ass past my mamas old house now and see a for sale sign they put one of them out front here but I tore that shit out the ground the city still gonna get they money though we gotta be out by tomorrow night damn nigga you might be my last cut they done took all 'cept this chair and these blades same ones I been using since '89 they still sound the same they still cut clean but they loud they sound like a bulldozer comin these blades been watchin all that black hair fall since we got here these blades been watchin all those black buildings fall since we got here niggas ain't got nowhere to go except under the ground my son got locked up fuckin with those packs trynna make money for the family we ain't been eatin ever since they built that salon for the white folks next door we ain't been eatin ever since the white families moved in and couldn't pronounce my son's name niggas hungry everything for sale out here everything got a price they gonna turn my mamas old house into a shoe store they gonna turn my mamas old house into a bakery they gonna bake shit that we can't even afford I'm gonna walk by and smell my mamas pies coming off the brick my stomach been eating itself for so long my stomach the only thing full on my whole body my girl been crying since our son got locked up my girl been crying so long we got a river in our backyard my nigga said that shit might take us to the promised land like I know what that shit mean like the promised land ain't courtright and livingston I ain't leavin my home nigga they gonna have to drag me through the streets they gonna have to pull me right off the porch I ain't goin out like I'm soft my daddy built that house my daddy built this hood my daddy got his hands all over this white shit and they don't even know it my son be sending letters from jail my son gotta come home to the same bedroom he grew up in I ain't leavin unless I bleed out right where they killed big mike you remember that nigga his moms live out west now they gettin all of us outta here swear to god swear to god I'mma be buried right here though nigga I'mma be buried right underneath another starbucks or some shit and I'mma be a ghost I'mma keep the hood safe after I die the o.g.'s ain't save us but shit my name still on the door for one more night nigga let me give you a cut 'fore you head back

THE CROWN AIN'T WORTH MUCH

Don't smoke / black!
Don't get smoked / black!
Don't smoke your lungs / black!
Police won't pull those guns / back!
Don't be black / smoke

on a back / road

they gonna push you in that cracked /road
they gonna claim another black / ghost
you get high enough they gonna say you asked for it
you get high enough you gonna lay on the asphalt
'til your blood runs back to where your mama stay
'til we pray over your feast for summer
you get high enough
the whole world gonna know your mama name

the whole world is going to know your mother's name

after your own falls off of her tongue for the last time

into the sweet brown soil that owns your hollow body

I know there's always gonna be a dead black body in summer

I know summer is a set of arms that never don't never end

until we run outta houses for the black angels in that new heaven

where every black grandma jesus to somebody

Sunday afternoon always on repeat

after the knees been pressed to that old wooden church floor and we prayed

for the black children climbing up that long ladder

and no one falls asleep to a chorus of bullets in the new heaven

and don't nobody turn on the news and see someone who got their baby's eyes in the new heaven

and it smell like chicken always in the pan even when chicken ain't in the pan and the song on the radio

always some song that you and your grandma know, and you are still alive in someone's mouth

I am still alive in my father's mouth
I can still watch him blow a thick cloud of it in the air
that blows south from our ohio porch where we are
talking about the trees but not their history
not the lives their branches have emptied
but how the one in the front yard must fall
so he can look out into another trembling dawn
and know that he lived another day in this country
its mouth wet for his sacrifice, and isn't that also justice
cutting into the husk of what once wore your ancestors as jewelry and
watching it fall. spending the new day staring at the blank space
it used to fill and washing your living black skin in the morning's warmth
isn't that also rebellion to stare into the horizon and not see a funeral
doesn't that also set fire to a country that wishes your children buried

In a country that wishes your children buried,

you do not wish a child on your children

you wish them loneliness. Or a lover, who is eager to keep an empty bedroom

I can't help but watch the black kids on the eastside playing

on a street where the cars still stop after a basketball

takes a bad bounce off the side of a rim and escapes the driveway

nostalgia is a gift for the living. When I say that I am growing old

I mean that I have lived long enough to fear death

I have been beckoned by a stone pressed into the cold earth

I can see what rests on the edge of my reflection / how I look so much

like my mother, who now looks like no one still tethered to the earth

this nomadic face, this blank slate eager to shake itself free

this legacy, eager to be given, yet no one wanting to carry its burden

as another shot fires off the back of the hoop / becoming swallowed by the sky

becoming swallowed by the sky was the only option when the police caught Jason
with two bricks outside the dollar store back in july '07, two years after Jason got his scholarship pulled
the day after he blew out his knee playing summer ball on the north courts where we used to hustle
white boys for whatever their mothers lined their pockets with
where we used to take food out of the mouths of boys who never considered a world where they would
not be fed. Who never had to come home from college with one good leg and one sick grandfather and
one whole hood being swallowed by shopping malls, and isn't this the story you were expecting? One
where I do not have to tell you that the hero is dead? I say a black boy's name in a poem and the boy
already begins to disappear from head to toe. I come from a place where no one goes *back* to jail. we
choose what box we will rot in. I am lucky that mine has windows. Pays me a fair wage. Gives me a week
off to attend a funeral. I once saw Jason make 12 shots in a row / I have played enough of the game to
know when it doesn't matter if you put up a hand / if you ask for mercy / I once saw Jason holding his
outstretched arms into the breeze of this violent machine while the net still trembled
from another gentle kiss

97

Ode to the gentle kiss

Ode to the violent machine / Ode to the violence

Ode to the endless scroll of names crawling out of my phone/ mummifying my bedroom

Ode to the bed / Ode to the glow of the telephone screen

Ode to the rage that pours from it

Ode to the night / ode to the nightmare / ode to not knowing which darkness will come for you next

Ode to sleep. Ode to not sleeping.

Ode to the cloak of sleeplessness.

Ode to lying about why you look so tired

Ode to watching yourself vanish on an endless loop with no trigger warning

Ode to the endless trigger / Ode to the endless warning / the one that says

they will not fight for you until you are gone

as long as you are a man / who does not love men

as long as you are smiling in at least one photo

head tilted, an avalanche of joy overflowing in your one mouth

I only have this one mouth.

I cannot make it into a graveyard for you anymore.

I just learned how to make room under my tongue for the name of someone who loves me

I blow it into the sky and it takes the shape of my mother's face.

I am running out of room for all of the other names.

I don't know how to go a day without them spilling out at my feet.

I say *Mike* and a cardinal lands on my shoulder.

I say *Trayvon* and a rainbow stretches over a city where it doesn't rain.

I say *Sandra* and a new tree grows in my father's front yard.

It stretches to the sky. It carries armfuls of light back to where he rests

and reminds him that I am still whole.

I am still whole.

I am still whole.

In another summer of black smoke.

THE STORY OF THE LAST PUNK ROCK SHOW BEFORE THE CITY TORE DOWN LITTLE BROTHER'S

Gets longer every time I tell it. It can stretch itself across a table for hours, depending on what diner the table is inside of, or the pooled money that can be thrown across the table's smooth face, or how much change we have left to romance the jukebox into playing something by someone who is no longer living. In this version, I tell you what you most want to hear: the sky lets a shower of fractured light leak through its teeth and fall onto our arms, still damp with the glitter that a guitarist threw from the front of the stage. In this version we are not swollen fat with grief. We did not stand in the storm on high street for two whole days and wish to drown. We moved because we could. The bitter rain did not split whatever youth we had left. In this version, there are no buildings high enough for a body to fall from and become a memory, a boundless winter grown ripe in a mother's bones. In this version, I tell you that it was always just music. I do not use words like "holy", or "church. I speak plain about the split lip. I speak of how the salt from a French fry stolen off of a pretty girl's plate fell into this canyon of blood and I still did not wince. I tell you that I sat in a cold shower at 3 a.m., washed the sweat off of my back with a hard bar of soap and prayed for no memory of this in the morning. I made room on my skin for the grief to sit, and nothing more. I name the wounds but do not discuss how they arrived. In this version, Everyone we love is still alive. In this version, I say *alive* and do not mean *I touched the face of my friend in a dream*. I say *alive* and mean *someone was there to pull me by the shirt when the boy's elbow glanced my face, and I did not fight until I wept, calling out a dead boy's name with each swing of a reckless fist*. I say *alive* and a sheet of ice appears in my bedroom. Once, the way we knew summer was over was when the fireflies stopped dancing around our heads, when the cicadas carried their songs south and left us to our unforgiving cold and we went to shows with no coats on, shivering together in a packed line. Every winter, I visit a new grave. Eventually, Ohio will run out of ground. And then what of the bodies? What land has arms large

enough to hold us all after we are gone, but still full of so much promise? In this version, we hid packs of cigarettes from our friends and stopped buying lighters. In this version, we still believe that drinking in smoke is the only thing that will kill us. In this version, a boy sprays *punk will never die* onto the brick wall outside and I do not tell him that I know death. I do not tell him that I have crawled into that hollow mouth and exited through the other side. I do not tell him that death is not when a city makes a strip mall out of where you bled once. That is the *other* death. The one that wears your name, but does not ask you to wear its own. The nostalgia is killing me again. In this version, I say *killing* and know that I will come back, still breathing, to my father. A remembered voice, a siren song of disappointment and still forgiveness. I say *killing* and I pull a long black feather from where the word grew underneath my tongue. It falls to the floor and becomes a torn jacket. In this version, I do not speak the name of the boy who wore the jacket across his breathless chest while he was carried, six of us on each side of a wooden box. Forgive me father, for I have made a suit of all these names I refuse to speak, and gone dancing in it. I have let all of me soak through it until it is a dark mess, falling from my shoulders. I keep handfuls of lighters only to press them into the blooming darkness when August makes another slow and hot exit. The seasons I remember most are the ones I never want to come again. And isn't this how each story starts? With a list of things we know we cannot take back? And, still. Everything has an end. This is where I tell you what I most want to hear myself: none of it was real. I am still sitting in a diner on the Eastside of Columbus and it has felt like summer for ten whole years. There is still a living mother, hovering over a sewing machine in the home I can always come back to. My name is still scrawled on the bathroom wall of a dive bar. The dive bar is still a dive bar. I am a forest of beginnings. I am never alone. I do not bury. I do not funeral. I can still look into mirrors. I do not see a chorus of ghosts. I do not cover my bedroom walls in posters of old punk bands to keep the ghosts out. I am at a diner and the table is full. No one is covered in dirt. The jukebox is still hungry for the silver that lines our pockets. Kurt Cobain is still singing *I'm so happy / 'cause today / I've found my friends...*
In this version, we are laughing loud enough to drown out the next line. Kurt sings

They're in my head
And I pretend not to feel winter moving in.

ACKNOWLEDGMENTS

Of course, my family: My father, my siblings. Laura, my loving and patient partner. This collection would not be possible without all of your intersections in my life.

Everyone at Button Poetry/Exploding Pinecone Press: Michael, Dylan, Sam, Anna, and the whole team. Thank you so much for believing in this project, even when I had no idea what I was doing.

My closest friends, who have gently and generously seen me through the entire life reflected in these poems: David, Meaghan, Ethan, Stephanie, Sam. You all are my people. Always.

The Columbus poetry community, and all of the poets within: Scott Woods, William Evans, Rose Smith, Steve Abbott, Rachel Wiley, Stephanee Killen, Vernell Bristow, Louise Robertson, Kidd, J.G., Ed Plunkett, Karen Scott, Alex Scott, Matthias Jackson, Joe Atticus Inch, Jordan McFall, Meg Freado, M. Shaw, Dave Nichols, Spike Cowell, Betsy Clark, Zach Hannah, Brandon Crittenden, Alexis Mitchell, Fayce Hammond, Aaron Alsop, Joy Sullivan, Madison Gibbs, Kim Brazwell, Jason Brazwell, Bill Hurley, Paula Lambert, Barb Fant, Izetta Thomas, Sidney Jones Jr, Kim Leddy, the Mosaic Students, Xavier Smith, Alex Caplinger, Quartez Harris, Hannah Stephenson, Maggie Smith, Is Said, Never Let Your Pen Dry, With Poetry, Writing Wrongs, Writer's Block, The Poetry Forum, The Ness, Paging Columbus, and Pen and Palette Always. Thank you all for providing the time, space, energy and work into this brilliant community that has forever kept me fed. Please keep the future of it strong.

The cohort of poets who push me to be better a better writer, and challenge me to be a better person: Danez Smith, Sarah Kay, Fatimah Asghar, Clint Smith, Eve Ewing, Nate Marshall, Franny Choi, Muggs Fogarty, Chrysanthemum Tran, Vatic, Emily O'Neill, Megan Falley, Jacob Rakovan, Cam Awkward-Rich, Hieu Nguyen, Aaron Samuels, Jayson Smith, José Olivarez aka Papi Two Times, Aziza Barnes, Adam Falkner, Mahogany Browne, Olivia Gatwood, Khadijah Queen, Javon Johnson, Jericho Brown, Kyle Dargan,

Joshua Bennett, Angel Nafis, Rachel McKibbens, Sabrina Benaim, David Winter, Raena Shirali, Paige Quiñones, Morgan Parker, Sam Sax, Julian Randall, Jacqui Germain, Phil Kaye, Ariana Brown, Sasha Banks, Omar Holmon, Shira Erlichman, Yasmin Belkhyr, Danniel, Schoonebeek, Nabila Lovelace, Jay Deshpande, Robbie Q, Jon Sands, Sam Rush, Chace Morris, Cassandra de Alba, Sophia Holtz, Zeke Russell, Charlotte Abotsi, Simone Beaubien, Jessica Rizkallah, Porsha O., Janae Johnson, Meaghan Ford, Tatyana Brown, Jeanann Verlee, Miles Walser, Safia Elhillo, Camille Rankine, Phillip B. Williams, Jerriod Avant, Mark Cugini, Paul Tran, Casey Rochetau, Anis Mojgani, Sam Mercer, McKendy Fils-Aime, Khary Jackson, Jamaal May, Geoff Kagan Trenchard, Desiree Dallagiacomo, Jonathan Mendoza, Siaara Freeman, Kieran Collier, Allison Truj, Anthony Ragler, Nicole Homer, Adam Levin, Melissa Lozada-Oliva, Derrick Carr, Sara Brickman, Gabriel Ramirez, Andrew Yim, Deonte Osayande, Sam Gordon, Justin Phillip Reed, Marty McConnell, Ocean Vuong, Desiree Bailey, Adam Hamze, Roger Reeves, Alex Dang, Dark Noise, Divine Fabrics, Darkmatter, Other Black Girl Collective, and so many more. Thank you all for lighting the path.

Stevie Edwards and everyone at Muzzle Magazine: Thank you so much for allowing me to work with you all. I have become such a better reader and writer due to my time with you all.

Places that have given me the space and time to do this work: Hurston-Wright, with special thanks to Terrance Hayes, Callaloo, Thurber House, and Columbus Arts Festival.

This book is dedicated to the memory. The memory of any moment you have loved or been in love, and the people who lived in that moment with you. For my mother, for the changing city I once knew and the one I love still, for Tyler, for Mike, for the barber shop, for Gina Blaurock, for MarShawn McCarrel. For anyone you miss.

Thank you for sharing this brief and fantastic life with me.

Thank you to the following journals who first gave versions of these poems a home:

Drunk in a Midnight Choir: "Ode to Pete Wentz, Ending in Tyler's Funeral," and "Ode to Drake, Ending With Blood in a Field"

Electric Cereal: "The Author Writes the First Draft of His Wedding Vows," and "At My First Punk Rock Show Ever"

Freezeray: "At the House Party Where We Found Out Whitney Houston Was Dead"

The Journal: "Ode to Kanye West, Ending in a Chain of Mothers Rising From The River," and "XVI"

Muzzle: "The Summer a Tribe Called Quest Broke Up"

The Offing: "On Hunger," and "I Don't Remember the Whole Summer When Do the Right Thing Dropped"

PEN American: "After The Cameras Leave, In Three Parts"

Sidekick Lit: "Dispatches from the Black Barbershop, Tony's Chair (2011)"

THIS: "On Melting," "Okay, I'm Finally Ready to Say I'm Sorry For That One Summer," and "Windsor Terrace, 1990"

Vinyl: "When We Were 13, Jeff's Father Left the Needle Down on a Journey Record Before Leaving the House One Morning and Never Coming Back," and "The Author Explains good kid, m.A.A.d. City to His White Friend While Driving Through Southeast Ohio"

Western Beefs: "USVvCuba," "Dispatches from the Black Barbershop, Tony's Chair (1996)," "The Music or The Misery," and "In Defense of Moist"

Winter Tangerine Review: "1995. After The Streetlights Drink Whatever Darkness is Left," "Ode To Jay-Z Ending in the Rattle of a Fiend's Teeth," "All of the Black Boys Finally Stopped Packing Switchblades," and "My Wife Says It's A Good Thing Humans Don't Hold Fear"

ABOUT THE AUTHOR

Hanif Abdurraqib is a poet and writer from the east side of Columbus, Ohio. He is a Callaloo Creative Writing fellow, and a columnist for MTV News. This is his first full-length collection of poems.

OTHER BOOKS
BY BUTTON POETRY